This book belongs to

Pass the Peas, Please

A Book of Manners

By Dina Anastasio
Illustrated by Katy Keck Arnsteen

WARNER JUVENILE BOOKS

A Warner Communications Company

New York

Suggested for ages 3–7.

Warner Juvenile Books Edition
Copyright © 1988 by Dina Anastasio and Katy Keck Arnsteen and RGA Publishing Group, Inc.
All rights reserved.

Warner Books, Inc., 666 Fifth Avenue, New York, NY 10103
Ⓦ A Warner Communications Company

Printed in the United States of America.
First Warner Juvenile Books Printing: April 1988
10 9 8 7 6 5 4 3 2 1

Library of Congress Cataloging-in-Publication Data

Anastasio, Dina.
  Pass the peas, please.

  Summary: Rhymed text and illustrations describe the
appropriate and polite behavior for many different
kinds of situations.
  [1. Behavior—Fiction. 2. Stories in rhyme]
I. Arnsteen, Katy Keck, ill. II. Title.
PZ8.3.A5294Pas 1988   [E]   87-18882
ISBN 1-55782-021-X

If you run over a sand castle
Created by your brother,
Kneel down and say, "I'm sorry."
Then just help him build another.

When you see someone who's different,
Don't laugh. It isn't fair.
He might think *you* are different,
But *he* doesn't point and stare.

If you're angry at a friend,
Don't punch or kick or shout.
Go for a walk and count to ten,
Then try to talk it out.

No one likes to lose a game,
But if you must, you must.
So if you lose, shake hands and say,
"We'll play again, I trust."

It's hard to keep a secret,
But secret telling's wrong.
Remember, friends who blab too much
Aren't friends for very long.

If your father's talking on the phone
When he should be playing ball,
Don't kick or sulk or whine, "Let's GO!"
That will not work at all.

Don't interrupt your uncle
When he's talking 'bout his car.
Even though it's boring—
Well, you know how uncles are!

When you're eating mashed potatoes,
And there's something you must say,
Please wait until you've swallowed.
The thought won't go away!

If your brother has a cupcake
That he's saving for tomorrow,
Don't take a bite, not even one,
Or he'll be filled with sorrow.

If your neighbor won't stop talking,
And you feel a yawn come on,
Put your mouth behind your fingers,
Until your yawn is gone.

Don't eat spaghetti with your knife,
Your fingers or a spoon.
Use your fork, although it's hard.
You'll catch on pretty soon.

When you're outside playing soccer,
And kick someone in the knee,
Don't tell him that he's in your way.
Say, "Sorry. Pardon me."

Don't play with Grandma's dishes
If your father has forbid it.
But if you do, and if they break,
Don't say your sister did it!

We all leave toys and clothes around.
It's O.K. just once or twice.
But if a king and queen should come to call,
They might not think it's nice.

When someone's in the bathroom,
And won't get out, don't worry.
Just knock and say, "I'm waiting.
I *must* come in. Please hurry."

Don't play the drums or sing a song
When somebody is sick.
Just tiptoe by and give a wave,
And say, "Please get well quick."

When your sister's busy practicing,
And you really want to hide,
Don't cover your ears or make a face.
Just smile and go outside.

Towels that are soggy
Will not dry someone's back.
So toss them in the laundry,
Or hang them on the rack.

When your sister gets a bicycle
And you just get a kite,
Don't say, "You like *her* better!"
Say, "Thank you. It's just right."

If a friend is having trouble,
And he falls and gives a yelp,
Don't laugh or point or call him names.
Say, "Are you hurt?" and "May I help?"

If there's something very special
That you'd really like to borrow,
Ask before you take it,
And bring it back tomorrow.

If your great-aunt gives you candy,
And your friends would like a lot,
It's nice to share a little,
Even though you'd rather not.

When you're going to a movie,
And the line is two blocks long,
Don't butt in front. Go to the end.
Then calmly hum a song.